VEGAN-

GW00457696

NUTRil

RECIPES

By

Celeste Jarabese

DISCLAIMER

LIMITS OF LIABILITY

Table of Contents

INTRODUCTION

This is a part of a series of NUTRiBULLET recipe book that focuses on **Vegan-Friendly** smoothie recipes.

Vegan refers to a person who doesn't include meat, poultry, seafood, fish, eggs and other animal products like cow's milk and other dairies in their diet. They focus mainly on plant-based food sources because they believe that it will keep their body organs healthy and also for longevity.

Fruits, both fresh and dried, were used in the recipes here as well as different kinds of vegetables, nuts, seeds and non-dairy liquid bases like tea, soy milk, soy yogurt, almond milk, juices, and coconut water.

The recipes in this book is created to meet the nutritional needs of Vegans by drinking healthy smoothies rich in essential nutrients such as carbohydrates, protein, fats, vitamins, and minerals. And since they are from plant sources they are also very rich in antioxidants. These antioxidants can help prevent cell damage often caused by free radicals.

To help Vegans further, the recipes in this book make use of "NUTRiBULLET Super food Extractor". It is an astounding machine that has the ability to release all the healthy components from your ingredients so you will be able to maintain a healthy body through proper nourishment.

Let's get it started! But before we proceed, I would like to thank you for purchasing and I hope that you will try and enjoy all the recipes in this book.

Happy reading!

Berry and Spinach Power Smoothie

Both berries and spinach have a wide range of nutrients, yielding a juice that can easily boost your immune system while having an amazing taste and being highly refreshing.

Preparation Time: 5 minutes
Total Time: 5 minutes
Yield: 1 serving

Ingredients
½ cup frozen blackberries
1 medium apple, cored and diced
1 handful spinach
2 tablespoons coconut milk
Coconut water to max line

Method
1.   Combine blackberries, apple, spinach, coconut milk, and coconut water in your Nutribullet and process until smooth and well blended.
2.   Pour the mixture in a glass of your choice and enjoy.

Avocado Carrot and Orange Smoothie

This healthy smoothie recipe with avocado, carrot, orange, and almond milk will provide your body with healthy fats and antioxidants known to prevent many diseases.

Preparation Time: 5 minutes
Total Time: 5 minutes
Yield: 1 serving

Ingredients
1 handful baby spinach
¼ medium avocados cut into small pieces
½ medium carrot, grated
½ medium orange, cut into segments
Almond milk to max line

Method
1.   Combine avocado, carrot, orange juice, and water in the tall glass. Process in the NutriBullet for 20 seconds or until smooth.
2.   Pour in a serving glass. Garnish with a slice of avocado, if desired.
3.   Serve and enjoy!

Berry and Kale Vegan Smoothie

How about a nutritious smoothie to start your day on a high note? This recipe is surely perfect for that due to its intense taste and amazing flavor. The berries bring plenty of antioxidants, while the kale boosts the fiber content, yielding a perfectly nourishing drink.

Preparation Time: 5 minutes
Total Time: 5 minutes
Yield: 1 serving

Ingredients

½ cup frozen mixed berries
1 handful kale
½ medium apple, cored and diced
1 teaspoon maple syrup
Water to max line

Method

1.   Place mixed berries, kale, apple, maple syrup, and water in the Nutribullet.
2.   Process for 20 seconds or until smooth.
3.   Transfer in a serving glass. Enjoy.

Green Asparagus Kiwi and Hemp Smoothie

Asparagus is incredibly healthy with its high nutritional content and there is no reason to not use it in a smoothie. Adding kiwifruit and hemp seeds improve the taste, consistency, and nutritional content.

Preparation Time: 5 minutes
Total Time: 5 minutes
Yield: 1 serving

Ingredients
½ cup asparagus tips
1 medium kiwi fruit
1 handful baby spinach
1 teaspoon hemp seeds
Rice milk to max line

Method
1.	Place asparagus tips, kiwifruit, baby spinach, hemp seeds, and rice milk in the Nutribullet.
2.	Process for 20 seconds or until smooth.
3.	Transfer in a serving glass. Enjoy.

Berry Beet and Coconut Smoothie

Fruits that have a strong color are loaded with antioxidants. The deeper the color, the more nutrients they have. Now you can see why this berry and beet smoothie combination is good for you.

Preparation Time: 5 minutes
Total Time: 5 minutes
Yield: 1 serving

Ingredients
½ cup wild berries
1 piece beetroot, cut into small pieces
1-2 ice cubes
Coconut water to max line

Method
1.   Place wild berries, beetroot, ice cubes, and coconut water in the Nutribullet.
2.   Process for 20-30 seconds or until smooth.
3.   Transfer in a serving glass. Enjoy.

Arugula Pineapple and Almond Smoothie

This green smoothie recipe made is with arugula, pineapple, and almond milk. If you want something that will give you energy and tummy friendly this the right one for you.

Preparation Time: 5 minutes
Total Time: 5 minutes
Yield: 1 serving

Ingredients

1 handful arugula or baby rocket
½ cup pineapple chunks
¾ cup almond milk
1-2 ice cubes

Method

1.   Combine arugula, pineapple, almond milk and ice in the tall glass.
2.   Process in the Nutribullet for 20 seconds or until mixture becomes smooth.
3.   Transfer in a serving glass. Enjoy.

Soy Berry and Banana Vegan Smoothie

This combination is a classic and it tastes great, being a thick and rich smoothie. Great to be served in the morning, before breakfast or in the afternoon, as a snack.

Preparation Time: 5 minutes
Total Time: 5 minutes
Yield: 1 serving

Ingredients
½ cup frozen strawberries
½ medium bananas
½ cup soy yogurt
Water to max line

Method
1.   Place strawberries, banana, soy yogurt, and water in the Nutribullet.
2.   Process for 20 seconds or until smooth.
3.   Transfer in a serving glass. Enjoy.

Berry Almond and Spinach Smoothie Recipe

This green smoothie recipe with fresh berries, spinach, and almond milk will do wonders to your health. It contains high amounts of fiber, vitamins and natural antioxidants that help fight against free radicals that can cause many degenerative diseases.

Preparation Time: 5 minutes
Total Time: 5 minutes
Yield: 1 serving

Ingredients
½ cup frozen strawberries, halved
¼ cup frozen blueberries
1 tablespoon Goji berries
1 cup spinach
Almond milk to max line

Method
1.   Place strawberries, blueberries, spinach, and almond milk into the tall glass. Process in the NutriBullet for 20 seconds or until combined well.
2.   Pour in a chilled glass. Garnish with fresh berries, if desired.
3.   Serve and enjoy!

Bell Pepper and Tomato Smoothie

Unlike fruits, vegetables have less sugar, but just as much nutrients if not even more and that makes them perfect for weight loss. This smoothie is rather savory, but it's simply delicious and very flavorful.

Preparation Time: 5 minutes
Total Time: 5 minutes
Yield: 1 serving

Ingredients

½ medium bell pepper, deseeded, sliced
2 medium tomatoes, diced
2 tablespoons lemon juice
1 teaspoon stevia
Water to max line

Method

1.   Place bell pepper, tomatoes, lemon juice, stevia, and water in the Nutribullet.
2.   Process for 20 seconds or until smooth.
3.   Transfer in a serving glass. Enjoy.

Bell Pepper Blueberry and Coconut Smoothie with Flax

Just like any other brightly colored fruits or vegetables, bell peppers are rich in antioxidants. They are mildly flavored too; it is definitely worth a try.

Preparation Time: 5 minutes
Total Time: 5 minutes
Yield: 1 serving

Ingredients

½ medium red bell pepper, deseeded and sliced
¾ cup frozen blueberries
½ medium ripe bananas
1 tablespoon flax seeds
Coconut water to max line

Method

1.   Combine all the ingredients in your Nutribullet and process 30-40 seconds or until well blended and smooth.
2.   Pour the drink in a glass of your choice and enjoy.

Beet Carrot and Lemon Blast

This healthy smoothie has a beautiful color and a rich nutritional content with its wide range of vitamins and antioxidants. It's great enjoyed in the morning it will help neutralize the other acids in your stomach or blood. The result is an increased energy level.

Preparation Time: 5 minutes
Total Time: 5 minutes
Yield: 1 serving

Ingredients

1medium beetroot, diced
½ medium carrot, diced
2 tablespoons lemon juice
Water to max line

Method

1.   Place beetroot, carrot, lemon juice, and water in the Nutribullet.
2.   Process for 20 seconds or until smooth.
3.   Transfer in a serving glass. Enjoy.

Spiced Beet Apple Cucumber and Sweet Potato Smoothie

Although slightly unusual to consume raw sweet potatoes, they represent one of the best sources of beta-carotene – a strong antioxidant.

Preparation Time: 5 minutes
Total Time: 5 minutes
Yield: 1 serving

Ingredients

1 medium beetroot, diced
½ medium apple, cored and diced
¼ medium cucumber, sliced
½ medium sweet potato, peeled and diced
½ teaspoon fresh ginger, grated
Water to max line

Method

1.   Place beetroot, apple, cucumber, sweet potato, ginger, and water in the Nutribullet.
2.   Process for 20-30 seconds or until smooth.
3.   Transfer in a serving glass. Enjoy.

Beet Red Cabbage and Grapefruit Smoothie

Although it only has just a few ingredients, this juice is loaded with antioxidants. I'm sure you would never expect the two main ingredients of this juice to be listed as some of the healthiest veggies out there, but they are.

Preparation Time: 5 minutes
Total Time: 5 minutes
Yield: 1 serving

Ingredients

1 medium beetroot, diced
2 red cabbage leaves, shredded
1 medium grapefruit, cut into segments
Water to max line

Method

1.   Place beetroot, red cabbage, grapefruit, and water in the Nutribullet.
2.   Process for 20 seconds or until smooth.
3.   Transfer in a serving glass. Enjoy.

Peach Pear and Almond Smoothie

This Vegan-friendly smoothie recipe is great for weight loss because it is high in fiber, but low in calories.

Preparation Time: 5 minutes
Total Time: 5 minutes
Yield: 1 serving

Ingredients
1 medium peach, diced
½ medium pear, cored and diced
½ cup almond milk
1-2 ice cubes

Method
1.   Place peach, pear, almond milk, and ice cubes in the Nutribullet.
2.   Process for 20 seconds or until smooth.
3.   Transfer in a serving glass. Enjoy.

Blueberry Pecan and Soy Smoothie

Blueberries are high in antioxidants and vitamins which makes this smoothie the perfect choice to fight off colds and flu during the cold season.

Preparation Time: 5 minutes
Total Time: 5 minutes
Yield: 1 serving

Ingredients
¾ cup frozen blueberries
½ cup soy milk
6 pecan nuts
Water to max line

Method
1.   Place blueberries, soy milk, pecan nuts, and water in the Nutribullet.
2.   Process for 20 seconds or until smooth.
3.   Transfer in a serving glass. Enjoy.

Beet and Blueberry Smoothie Recipe

A combination of beet, blueberries, and orange. This smoothie recipe is loaded with folate and vitamin C.

Preparation Time: 5 minutes
Total Time: 5 minutes
Yield: 1 serving

Ingredients

1 piece beetroot, diced
½ cup blueberries
½ cup orange juice
2 ice cubes
Water to max line

Method

1.   Place beetroot, blueberries, orange juice, ice, and water in the Nutribullet.
2.   Process for 20-30 seconds or until smooth.
3.   Transfer in a serving glass. Enjoy.

Acai Berry Banana and Rice Smoothie

This delightful smoothie recipe made with acai berries, banana and rice milk is loaded with good for you nutrients to keep you healthy and energized.

Preparation Time: 5 minutes
Total Time: 5 minutes
Yield: 1 serving

Ingredients

½ cup acai berries
½ medium bananas
2/3 cup rice milk
2-3 ice cubes

Method

1.   In the tall glass, place the acai berries, banana, and rice milk. Process in the NutriBullet for 20-30 seconds or until smooth.
2.   Pour mixture in a tall glass with ice. Garnish with a few berries or mint sprig, if desired.
3.   Serve and enjoy!

Avocado Oat and Orange Juice

This delightful smoothie made with avocado, oats, and orange is naturally rich in healthy fats, vitamin C, and fiber which support normal functioning of the body organs leading to good health.

Preparation Time: 5 minutes
Total Time: 5 minutes
Yield: 1 serving

Ingredients
¼ medium avocado, diced
2 tablespoons steel-cut oats
½ cup fresh orange juice
1 teaspoon agave nectar
Water to max line

Method
1.   Place avocado, oats, orange juice, agave nectar, and water in the tall glass. Process in the NutriBullet for 20-30 seconds or until it is smooth.
2.   Pour mixture in a chilled glass. Garnish with a slice of orange, if desired.
3.   Serve and enjoy!

Almond Tropical Smoothie

This healthy and delicious smoothie with tropical and almond flavors is made with mango, banana, pineapple, and almond milk. It is loaded with nutrients that can keep you going for a longer period of time.

Preparation Time: 5 minutes
Total Time: 5 minutes
Yield: 1 serving

Ingredients
½ cup mango, diced
½ cup pineapple, diced
½ medium banana, sliced
½ cup almond milk
Water to max line

Method
1.   Combine the mango, pineapple, banana, and almond milk in the tall glass. Process in the NutriBullet for 20 seconds or until becomes smooth and creamy.
2.   Pour mixture in a serving glass. Garnish with a small slice of mango or pineapple, if desired.
3.   Serve and enjoy!

Apple Kiwi and Coconut Smoothie

Both apple and kiwi are considered as wonder fruits because of their high content of vitamins, minerals, and antioxidants. This smoothie will boost your immune system as well as your energy when you most need it.

Preparation Time: 5 minutes
Total Time: 5 minutes
Yield: 1 serving

Ingredients
1 medium green apple, cored and diced
1 medium kiwi fruit, sliced
2 ice cubes
Coconut water to max line

Method
1.   Combine green apple, kiwi, ice, and coconut water in the tall glass. Process in the NutriBullet for 20-30 seconds or until mixture becomes smooth.
2.   Transfer mixture in serving glass.
3.   Serve and enjoy!

Apple and Lime Chilled Smoothie

They say 'an apple a day keeps the doctor away'. It's true if we look into the high nutritional profile of apples.

Preparation Time: 5 minutes
Total Time: 5 minutes
Yield: 1 serving

Ingredients
1medium green apple, cored and diced
1 tablespoon lime juice
½ cup crushed ice
½ cup almond milk
1 teaspoon maple syrup
Pinch of cinnamon

Method
1.   Combine apple, lime juice, ice
almond milk, maple syrup, and cinnamon
in the tall glass. Process in the NutriBullet
for 20 seconds or until mixture becomes
smooth and creamy.
2.   Transfer mixture in serving glass.
3.   Serve and enjoy!

Apple Berry Ginger Blast Smoothie

This healthy and delicious smoothie with apple and strawberries has a mild twist to it because of the addition of ginger. Same with the nutritious berries and ginger which contain substances that provides the body with many health benefits.

Preparation Time: 5 minutes
Total Time: 5 minutes
Yield: 1 serving

Ingredients
1 medium apple
½ cup frozen strawberries
½ teaspoon ginger, grated
1 cup rice milk

Method
1.   Combine the apple, strawberries, ginger, and rice milk in the tall glass. Process in the NutriBullet for 20 seconds or until smooth and creamy.
2.   Pour in a chilled glass. Garnish with few strawberries and mint sprig, if desired.
3.   Serve and enjoy!

Fruit and Veggie Green Power Smoothie

This tasty fruit and veggie smoothie recipe is good for breakfast or snack it is loaded with powerful antioxidants that can fight diseases.

Preparation Time: 5 minutes
Total Time: 5 minutes
Yield: 1 serving

Ingredients

2 lettuce leaves, torn
1 handful spinach leaves
1 medium apple, cut into small pieces
2 tablespoons lime juice
1 teaspoon maple syrup
Water to max line

Method

1.   Place lettuce, spinach, apple, lime juice, maple syrup, and coconut water in the Nutribullet.
2.   Process for 20 seconds or until smooth.
3.   Transfer in a serving glass. Enjoy.

Banana Mango and Coconut Smoothie

A perfect blend of flavors from the banana, mango, and coconut.

Preparation Time: 5 minutes
Total Time: 5 minutes
Yield: 1 serving

Ingredients

½ medium bananas cut into small pieces
½ cup mango, diced
2 tablespoons coconut milk
1-2 ice cubes
Coconut water to max line

Method

1.   Place banana, mango, coconut milk, ice cubes, and coconut water in the Nutribullet.
2.   Process for 20-30 seconds or until smooth.
3.   Transfer in a serving glass. Enjoy.

Healthy Fennel Pear and Pineapple Smoothie

Fennel is a great ingredient in smoothies because it helps with digestion and toxin elimination. Plus, combined with pear and pineapple, it taste delicious as well.

Preparation Time: 5 minutes
Total Time: 5 minutes
Yield: 1 serving

Ingredients

¼ medium fennel bulb, shredded
1 medium pear, cored and diced
½ cup pineapple juice
¼ cup crushed ice

Method

1.   Place fennel, pear, pineapple juice, and crushed ice in the Nutribullet.
2.   Process for 20-30 seconds or until smooth.
3.   Transfer in a serving glass with ice. Enjoy.

Coco Moringa Smoothie

A blend of most healthy ingredients, just a simple and quick quench loaded with essential nutrients.

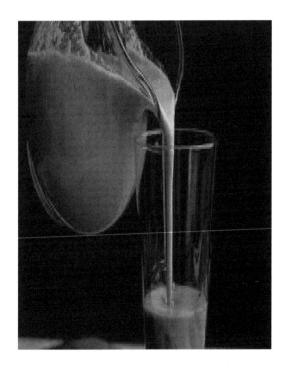

Preparation Time: 5 minutes
Total Time: 5 minutes
Yield: 1 serving

Ingredients

½ cup pineapple chunks
1/8 medium avocado, sliced
1 tablespoon moringa powder
Coconut water to max line

Method

1.   Place pineapple, avocado, moringa, and coconut in the Nutribullet.
2.   Process for 20 seconds or until smooth.
3.   Transfer in a serving glass with ice. Enjoy.

Garlic Celery and Apple Blast

It is well known the fact that garlic is one of the most efficient natural antibiotics; it can also strengthen your immune system. Celery and apple not only improves taste, but also add vitamins and minerals to your drink.

Preparation Time: 5 minutes
Total Time: 5 minutes
Yield: 1 serving

Ingredients

2 celery stalks, diced
1 medium apple, cored and diced
1 clove garlic
2 tablespoons lemon juice
1 teaspoon stevia
Water to max line

Method

1.   Place celery, apple, garlic, lemon juice, stevia, and water in the Nutribullet.
2.   Process for 10-15 seconds or until smooth.
3.   Transfer in a serving glass. Enjoy.

Celery Pineapple and Soy Smoothie

The health benefits of celery are too important to ignore. Celery is rich in vitamin C, folate, fiber and other antioxidants which your body needs to function properly.

Preparation Time: 5 minutes
Total Time: 5 minutes
Yield: 1 serving

Ingredients
2 celery stalks, diced
½ cup pineapple chunks
½ cup soy yogurt
Water to max line
Dash of nutmeg

Method
1.   Combine all the ingredients in your Nutribullet and pulse for 15-20 seconds or until well blended.
2.   Pour in a chilled glass and enjoy.

Papaya Carrot and Coconut Smoothie

Both papaya and carrots are high in beta-carotene, one of the most powerful antioxidants. They can also help detoxify the body from toxins.

Preparation Time: 5 minutes
Total Time: 5 minutes
Yield: 1 serving

Ingredients
½ cup papaya, cubed
½ medium carrot, cubed
½ cup coconut water
Dash of nutmeg, ground
1-2 ice cubes

Method
1.   Combine the ingredients in your Nutribullet and process for 20-30 seconds until well blended and smooth.
2.   Pour in a glass of your choice. Garnish with a slice of papaya.
3.   Enjoy.

Pineapple Avocado and Lime Smoothie

This healthy smoothie recipe with pineapple, avocado, and lime will provide your body with fiber, healthy fats and carbohydrates which you need for more stable source of energy.

Preparation Time: 5 minutes
Total Time: 5 minutes
Yield: 1 serving

Ingredients
½ cup pineapple chunks
¼ medium avocados cut into small pieces
1 tablespoon lime juice
1 teaspoon raw sugar
Water to max line

Method
1.   Combine avocado, coconut milk, lime juice, raw sugar, and coconut water in the tall glass.
2.   Process in the NutriBullet for 20 seconds or until smooth.
3.   Pour in a serving glass. Garnish with a small slice of avocado or lime, if desired.
4.   Serve and enjoy!

Mixed Berry Banana and Green Tea Blast

A delicious and healthy smoothie made of mixed berries, banana, and green tea.

Preparation Time: 5 minutes
Total Time: 5 minutes
Yield: 1 serving

Ingredients
½ cup frozen mixed berries
½ medium bananas
½ medium cucumbers
Freshly brewed green tea to max line

Method
1.   Combine mixed berries, banana, blueberries, cucumber, and green tea in the tall glass.
2.   Process in the NutriBullet for 20 seconds or until smooth.
3.   Pour in a serving glass. Garnish with a small a few berries, if desired.
4.   Serve and enjoy!

Green Banana Pineapple and Chia Smoothie

This green smoothie recipe made with banana, pineapple, coconut water and chia seeds are great for an afternoon pick me up.

Preparation Time: 5 minutes
Total Time: 5 minutes
Yield: 1 serving

Ingredients
1 handful kale
1 medium banana, sliced
½ cup pineapple chunks
1 teaspoon chia seeds

Method
1.   Combine kale, banana, pineapple, and chia seeds in the tall glass.
2.   Process in the NutriBullet for 20 seconds or until smooth.
3.   Pour in a serving glass. Garnish with a slice of pineapple, if desired.
4.   Serve and enjoy!

Mixed Green Avocado and Mango Smoothie

This smoothie recipe with spinach, lettuce, parsley, avocado, and mango is perfect for those who want to detoxify their bodies from unwanted toxins.

Preparation Time: 5 minutes
Total Time: 5 minutes
Yield: 1 serving

Ingredients
1 handful of spinach leaves, torn
2 pieces lettuce leaves, torn
2 tablespoon parsley, coarsely chopped
1/8 medium avocado
½ cup mango, diced
Water to max line

Method
1.   Place spinach, lettuce, parsley, avocado, mango, and water in the tall glass. Process in the NutriBullet for 20 seconds or until combined well.
2.   Pour in a serving glass. Garnish with parsley sprig, if desired.
3.   Serve and enjoy!

Minty Cantaloupe Oat Almond Smoothie

This smoothie recipe with cantaloupe, oatmeal, and almond milk is so wonderful that you will want to make over and over. It is also rich in fiber, vitamins and minerals for healthy heart.

Preparation Time: 5 minutes
Total Time: 5 minutes
Yield: 1 serving

Ingredients
¾ cup cantaloupe, cubed
¼ cup oatmeal
2/3 cup almond milk
Fresh mint sprig

Method
1.   Combine cantaloupe, oatmeal, almond milk, and 1 mint sprig in the tall glass. Process in the NutriBullet for 20 seconds or until it becomes smooth.
2.   Pour in a serving glass. Garnish with a small slice of cantaloupe and mint sprig, if desired.
3.   Serve and enjoy!

Minty Banana Mango Soy Smoothie

This a cool and refreshing beverage made with banana, mango, soy milk and mint. A must have drink when the weather is very hot.

Preparation Time: 5 minutes
Total Time: 5 minutes
Yield: 1 serving

Ingredients
½ medium bananas cut into small pieces
½ cup mango, cut into cubes
¾ cup soy milk, vanilla flavor
1 fresh mint sprig

Method
1.   Combine banana, mango, soy milk, and mint in the tall glass. Place and process in the NutriBullet for 20 seconds or until becomes smooth.
2.   Pour in a serving glass. Garnish with a small slice of mango and mint sprig, if desired.
3.   Serve and enjoy!

Melon Orange and Soy Smoothie

If you are looking for a healthy and tasty beverage for breakfast or afternoon snack this is the perfect recipe for you. This awesome smoothie is made with melon, orange, and soy milk.

Preparation Time: 5 minutes
Total Time: 5 minutes
Yield: 1 serving

Ingredients

¾ cup melon, diced
½ medium orange, cut into segments
½ cup soy milk
1-2 ice cubes

Method

1.   Combine melon, orange, soy milk, and ice in the tall glass. Process in the NutriBullet for 20-30 seconds or until mixture becomes smooth and creamy.
2.   Pour in a serving glass. Garnish with a small slice of melon or orange, if desired.
3.   Serve and enjoy!

Banana Melon and Almond Vegan Smoothie

Although the combination may sound surprising, the final drink is absolutely delicious and refreshing and it has enough nutrients to keep you full for a long period of time.

Preparation Time: 5 minutes
Total Time: 5 minutes
Yield: 1 serving

Ingredients

½ medium bananas cut into small pieces
¾ cup melon, cubed
¾ cup almond milk
1 tablespoon wheat germ

Method

1.   Combine banana, melon, almond milk, and wheat germ in your Nutribullet and process until smooth and creamy.
2.   Pour in a serving glass and enjoy.

Kiwi Lime and Coconut Summer Smoothie

During those hot summer days all you want is a refreshing drink and this smoothie fits right in with its fresh flavor and distinctive taste.

Preparation Time: 5 minutes
Total Time: 5 minutes
Yield: 1 serving

Ingredients
1 medium kiwifruit, sliced
1 tablespoon lime juice
1 tablespoon coconut milk
1 teaspoon maple syrup
1-2 ice cubes
Coconut water to max line

Method
1.   Place kiwifruit, lime juice, coconut milk, maple syrup, ice and coconut water in the Nutribullet.
2.   Process for 20-30 seconds or until smooth.
3.   Transfer in a serving glass and enjoy.

Lime Celery Spinach and Coconut Blast

This smoothie recipe is loaded with potassium, calcium, iron and loads of antioxidants and that makes it an excellent juice for your detox programs as it will help your body and blood eliminate the toxins.

Preparation Time: 5 minutes
Total Time: 5 minutes
Yield: 1 serving

Ingredients
2 celery stalks, diced
2 tablespoons lime juice
1 handful spinach
1 teaspoon stevia
Coconut water to max line

Method
1.   Place celery, lime juice, spinach, stevia, and coconut water in the Nutribullet.
2.   Process for 20-30 seconds or until smooth.
3.   Transfer in a serving glass and enjoy.

Tomato Lettuce and Orange Smoothie

Found all year around, tomatoes are rich in vitamins, minerals, and antioxidants. This smoothie can help boost your immune system to fight illness.

Preparation Time: 5 minutes
Total Time: 5 minutes
Yield: 1 serving

Ingredients
1cup cherry tomatoes, halved
2 lettuce leaves
½ cup fresh orange juice
1 teaspoon agave nectar
Water to max line

Method
1.   Place tomatoes, lettuce, orange, agave nectar, and water in the Nutribullet.
2.   Process for 20 seconds or until smooth.
3.   Transfer in a serving glass.
4.   Enjoy.

Radish Kale and Grape Smoothie

A healthy smoothie made with radish, kale, and grapes that is good for breakfast or snack.

Preparation Time: 5 minutes
Total Time: 5 minutes
Yield: 1 serving

Ingredients
1 medium radish, sliced
1 handful kale
¾ cup seedless grapes
Coconut water to max line

Method
1.   Place radish, kale, grapes, and coconut water in the Nutribullet.
2.   Process for 20 seconds or until smooth.
3.   Transfer in a serving glass.
4.   Enjoy.

Spinach Pear and Kombucha Smoothie with Chia

Kombucha tea is good on its own, but combined with some leafy greens and berries would yield a wonderful drink.

Preparation Time: 5 minutes
Total Time: 5 minutes
Yield: 1 serving

Ingredients
1 handful spinach
1 medium pear, cored and diced
1-2 ice cubes
1 teaspoon raw sugar
Kombucha tea to max line

Method
1.   Place spinach, pear, ice, raw sugar, and Kombucha in the Nutribullet.
2.   Process for 20 seconds or until smooth.
3.   Transfer in a serving glass.
4.   Enjoy.

Peach Pineapple and Almond Smoothie

This healthy smoothie will boost your metabolism and give you energy while providing you with plenty of fiber, vitamins, minerals, and antioxidants.

Preparation Time: 5 minutes
Total Time: 5 minutes
Yield: 1 serving

Ingredients
1 medium peach, diced
½ cup pineapple chunks
½ cup almond milk
1-2 ice cubes

Method
1.   Combine peach, pineapple, almond milk, and ice in a Nutribullet and process for 30-40 seconds or until well blended and smooth.
2.   Pour in a glass and enjoy.

Black Currant Soy and Flaxseed Smoothie

The healthy smoothie recipe is rich in fiber, vitamins, minerals, and antioxidants for optimal health.

Preparation Time: 5 minutes
Total Time: 5 minutes
Yield: 1 serving

Ingredients
½ cup black currants
½ cup soy milk
1 teaspoon flaxseeds
1 teaspoon agave nectar
1-2 ice cubes
Water to max line

Method
1.   Combine black currants, soy milk, flaxseeds, agave nectar, ice cubes, and water in a Nutribullet and process for 20-30 seconds or until well blended and smooth.
2.   Pour in a glass and enjoy.

Banana Pineapple and Coconut Smoothie

Banana when combined with coconut yields a rich smoothie that can boost your energy.

Preparation Time: 5 minutes
Total Time: 5 minutes
Yield: 1 serving

Ingredients
1 medium banana
½ cup pineapple chunks
2 tablespoons coconut cream
Coconut water to max line

Method
1.   Place all the ingredients in your Nutribullet and process 20 seconds or until the smoothie is well blended.
2.   Pour in a glass of your choice Garnish with a slice of pineapple, if desired.

Cherry Almond and Oat Smoothie with Hemp Seed

This Vegan-friendly smoothie with cherries, almond, banana, and oats makes a great breakfast or snack.

Preparation Time: 5 minutes
Total Time: 5 minutes
Yield: 1 serving

Ingredients

½ cup fresh cherries, pitted
½ medium bananas cut into small pieces
2/3 cup almond milk
1-2 ice cubes

Method

1.   Place cherries, banana, almond milk, ice cubes, and water in the Nutribullet.
2.   Process for 20-30 seconds or until smooth.
3.   Transfer in a serving glass. Enjoy.

Avocado Honeydew and Pumpkin Seed Smoothie

A sweet and creamy smoothie made with avocado, honeydew, almond milk, and pumpkin seeds.

Preparation Time: 5 minutes
Total Time: 5 minutes
Yield: 1 serving

Ingredients

¾ cup honeydew melon, cubed
1/8 medium ripe avocado, sliced
2 tablespoons pumpkin seeds
Almond milk to max line

Method

1.   Place honeydew, avocado, pumpkin seeds, and almond milk in the Nutribullet.
2.   Process for 20 seconds or until smooth. Garnish with a slice of honeydew melon, if desired.
3.   Transfer in a serving glass. Enjoy.

Healthy Citrus Spinach and Soy Smoothie

This Vegan-friendly smoothie made with citrus fruits, spinach and soy yogurt makes a yummy breakfast or snack on the go!

Preparation Time: 5 minutes
Total Time: 5 minutes
Yield: 1 serving

Ingredients

1 handful spinach, torn
1/2 cup orange, peeled, cut into segments
1 tablespoon lemon juice
2/3 cup soy yogurt, vanilla flavour
Water to max line

Method

1.   Place spinach, orange, lemon juice, soy yogurt, and water into the tall glass. Process in the NutriBullet for 10-12 seconds or until combined well.
2.   Pour in a chilled glass. Garnish with a slice of lemon or orange, if desired
3.   Serve and enjoy!

Spinach Banana and Coco Smoothie

This healthy drink is made with 3 super foods - spinach, banana, and coconut. It is loaded with nutrients that can help lower blood sugar level.

Preparation Time: 5 minutes
Total Time: 5 minutes
Yield: 1 serving

Ingredients
1 handful baby spinach
1 small frozen banana, cut into small pieces
2 tablespoon coconut milk
1 teaspoon chia seeds
Coconut water to max line

Method
1.   Combine the spinach, banana, coconut milk, chia seeds, and coconut water in the tall glass. Process in the NutriBullet for 20 seconds or until smooth.
2.   Pour in a chilled glass. Serve and enjoy!

Healthy Apple Banana and Soya Smoothie

This healthy smoothie recipe with apple, banana, and soya milk makes a fantastic breakfast or in between snack. Both apple and banana provides the body with great amounts of vitamins, minerals, and fiber for a fit body!

Preparation Time: 5 minutes
Total Time: 5 minutes
Yield: 1 serving

Ingredients

½ medium green apple, cored and cut into small pieces
½ medium frozen bananas cut into small pieces
¾ cup soya milk
¼ teaspoon cinnamon, ground
¼ teaspoon nutmeg, ground

Method

1.   Place apple, banana, soya milk, and cinnamon in the tall glass. Process in the NutriBullet for 10-12 seconds or until smooth and creamy.
2.   Transfer mixture in a serving glass. Sprinkle with nutmeg on top.
3.   Serve and enjoy!

Healthy Almond Lychee Smoothie Recipe

This healthy smoothie recipe with lychees, banana, and almond milk is rich in potassium and B-vitamins which is good for heart health!

Preparation Time: 5 minutes
Total Time: 5 minutes
Yield: 1 serving

Ingredients

4 pieces lychees, peeled, chopped
1 frozen banana, cut into small pieces
½ cup almond milk
Water to max line
Fresh mint sprig, for garnish

Method

1.   Place lychees, banana, almond milk, and water in the tall glass. Process in the NutriBullet for 10-15 seconds or until combined well.
2.   Pour in a chilled glass. Garnish with mint sprig.
3.   Serve and enjoy!

Orange Mango and Mint Smoothie

This smoothie recipe with orange, mango, rice milk, and mint is so delicious and good for you because it contains many important nutrients.

Preparation Time: 5 minutes
Total Time: 5 minutes
Yield: 1 serving

Ingredients
1 medium orange, cut into segments
½ cup mango, diced
½ cup rice milk
¼ cup crushed ice
1 mint sprig

Method
1.   Combine all the ingredients in your Nutribullet and process for 20 seconds or until the drink is smooth and well blended.
2.   Pour in a chilled glass. Garnish with a slice of orange or mango.
3.   Enjoy.

Kiwi Cucumber Lemon and Coconut Blast

Packed with vitamin C and antioxidants, this smoothie recipe is a real treat!

Preparation Time: 5 minutes
Total Time: 5 minutes
Yield: 1 serving

Ingredients

1 medium kiwifruit, sliced
½ medium cucumber, diced
2 tablespoons lemon juice
½ teaspoon lemon zest
1 teaspoon stevia
Coconut water to max line

Method

1.   Place kiwifruit, cucumber, lemon juice, lemon zest, stevia, and coconut water in the Nutribullet.
2.   Process for 20 seconds or until smooth.
3.   Transfer in a serving glass. Enjoy.

Green Grape Banana and Soy Smoothie

This green smoothie recipe is made with banana, soy milk, and green grapes. It is loaded with potassium which helps in fluid balance in the body and also good for the heart.

Preparation Time: 5 minutes
Total Time: 5 minutes
Yield: 1 serving

Ingredients

½ cup green grapes, seedless
½ medium bananas cut into small pieces
2/3 cup soy milk
1-2 ice cubes

Method

1.   Place the green grapes, banana, soy milk, and ice cubes in the tall glass. Process in the NutriBullet for 20-30 seconds or until becomes smooth and creamy.
2.   Pour in a serving glass. Garnish with fresh grapes, if desired.
3.   Serve and enjoy!

Spinach Honeydew Melon and Soy Smoothie

This is a great tasting smoothie made with spinach, honeydew melon, and soy milk. It will help you revitalize your energy for better performance at school, work, or play!

Preparation Time: 5 minutes
Total Time: 5 minutes
Yield: 1 serving

Ingredients
1 handful spinach, torn
¾ cup cantaloupe melon
2/3 cup soy milk, unsweetened
¼ cup crushed ice

Method
1.   Place spinach, cantaloupe, soy milk, and crushed ice in the tall glass. Process in the NutriBullet for 20 seconds or until mixture becomes smooth.
2.   Pour in a serving glass with ice. Garnish with a small chunk of melon, if desired.
3.   Enjoy!

Spiced Pumpkin Apple and Coconut Smoothie

Pumpkin is a good source of fiber and beta-carotene. This smoothie recipe combines pumpkin with apple, cinnamon, and coconut for a delicious and nutritious drink.

Preparation Time: 5 minutes
Total Time: 5 minutes
Yield: 1 serving

Ingredients

½ cup pumpkin puree
1 medium apple, cored and diced
½ cup almond milk
Pinch cinnamon, ground
Ice cubes to serve

Method

1.   Combine pumpkin puree, apple, almond milk, and cinnamon in your Nutribullet.
2.   Process until well blended, about 20 seconds or more if needed.
3.   Pour the drink in a serving glass with ice cubes.
4.   Enjoy.

Strawberry Soy and Rhubarb Smoothie

This smoothie with strawberry, soy milk, and rhubarb is a great drink for the summer.

Preparation Time: 5 minutes
Total Time: 5 minutes
Yield: 1 serving

Ingredients

½ cup frozen strawberries, halved
½ cup rhubarb, diced
½ cup soy milk
2 tablespoon wheat germ

Method

1.   Combine strawberries, rhubarb, soy milk, and wheat germ in your Nutribullet and process for 20-30 seconds or until the drink is smooth and well blended.
2.   Pour in a serving glass. Enjoy.

Spiced Protein Almond and Banana Smoothie

Power-up with this fiber-rich smoothie recipe! It is made with pea protein powder, almonds, banana, and cardamom. Great drink for fitness enthusiasts or body builders.

Preparation Time: 5 minutes
Total Time: 5 minutes
Yield: 1 serving

Ingredients
1 scoop pea protein powder
½ medium bananas cut into small pieces
6 pieces dry roasted almonds
Water to max line
Dash of cardamom, ground

Method
1.   Place pea protein powder, banana, almonds, water, and cardamom in the tall glass. Process in your NutriBullet for 20 seconds or until combined well.
2.   Pour in a chilled glass. Sprinkle with cardamom. Garnish with slivered almonds, if desired.
3.   Serve and enjoy!

Papaya Orange Shake with Cinnamon

This mildly spiced smoothie recipe made with papaya, orange, maple syrup and cinnamon is beneficial for people with digestive issues.

Preparation Time: 5 minutes
Total Time: 5 minutes
Yield: 1 serving

Ingredients
½ cup ripe papaya, diced
1 medium orange, cut into segments
1 tablespoon wheat germ
¼ teaspoon cinnamon, ground
1 teaspoon maple syrup
Water to max line

Method
1.   Place the papaya, orange, wheat germ, cinnamon, maple syrup, and water in the tall glass. Process in the NutriBullet for 20 seconds or until it becomes smooth.
2.   Pour in a chilled tall glass. Garnish with a slice of orange, if desired.
3.   Serve and enjoy!

Apple Cucumber and Cauliflower Smoothie

This healthy green beverage is made with apple, cucumber, cauliflower, lime juice, and stevia. A drink that is loaded with nutrients and antioxidants that will keep you protected against illnesses.

Preparation Time: 5 minutes
Total Time: 5 minutes
Yield: 1 serving

Ingredients

1 medium apple, peeled, cored, cut into
small pieces
½ medium cucumber, diced
4 cauliflower florets
1 tablespoon lime juice
1 teaspoon stevia
Water to max line

Method

1.   Combine the apple, cucumber,
cauliflower, lime juice, stevia, and water
in the tall glass.
2.   Process in the NutriBullet for 20
seconds or until smooth.
3.   Pour in a chilled glass. Garnish
with a slice of apple or lime, if desired.
4.   Serve and enjoy!

Soy Yogurt Spinach Smoothie with Raisins

This green smoothie recipe with soy yogurt, spinach, and raisins is a very nice drink for a morning or afternoon snack. It will provide your body with the right amount nutrients it needs to keep you healthy and strong.

Preparation Time: 5 minutes
Total Time: 5 minutes
Yield: 1 serving

Ingredients

1 handful spinach, torn
½ cup soy yogurt
½ cup soy milk, unsweetened
2 tablespoon raisins

Method

1.   Combine spinach, soy yogurt, soy milk and raisins in the tall glass. Process in the NutriBullet for 20 seconds or until it becomes smooth.
2.   Pour in a serving glass. Garnish with spinach or a few raisins, if desired.
3.   Serve and enjoy!

Green Almond Smoothie with Sunflower Seeds

This smoothie promotes stronger immune system and lowers blood pressure as well as cholesterol.

Preparation Time: 5 minutes
Total Time: 5 minutes
Yield: 1 serving

Ingredients

2 celery stalks, diced
2 tablespoons parsley, chopped
2 tablespoons sunflower seeds
½ cup almond milk

Method

1.   Place celery, parsley, sunflower seeds, and almond milk in the tall glass. Process in the Nutribullet for 10-15 seconds or until smooth.
2.   Pour mixture in a serving glass. Garnish with parsley, if desired.
3.   Enjoy.

Kale Peach and Almond Smoothie

This is a wonderful green smoothie recipe made with kale, peach, almond milk, and agave nectar will give you energy to withstand busy day.

Preparation Time: 5 minutes
Total Time: 5 minutes
Yield: 1 serving

Ingredients
1 handful kale, torn
1 medium peach, pitted and diced
¾ cup almond milk, unsweetened
1 teaspoon agave nectar
1-2 ice cubes

Method
1.   Combine kale, peach, almond milk, and agave nectarine the tall glass. Process in the NutriBullet for 20 seconds or until mixture becomes smooth.
2.   Transfer mixture in a serving glass with ice. Garnish with a small slice of peach, if desired.
3.   Serve and enjoy!

Silken Mango Papaya Protein Blast

Try this awesome blend of yellow fruits and tofu for a protein and fiber-rich breakfast or snack on the go. A refreshing summertime drink everyone will surely love!

Preparation Time: 5 minutes
Total Time: 5 minutes
Yield: 1 serving

Ingredients

½ cup mango, diced
½ cup papaya, diced
½ cup silken tofu
2 lettuce leaves, torn
½ teaspoon fresh ginger grated
Coconut water to max line

Method

1.   Place mango, papaya, tofu, lettuce, ginger, and coconut water in the tall glass. Process in the NutriBullet for 20 seconds or until combined well.
2.   Pour in a chilled glass. Garnish with a small slice of mango or papaya with mint sprig.
3.   Serve and enjoy!

Tip - You can also use ground cinnamon or cardamom to replace fresh ginger in this recipe.

Healthy Peanut Butter Smoothie with Chia

It's very easy to transform your peanut butter into a delicious and nutritious drink. All it takes is a few additional ingredients to end up with a perfect breakfast drink or snack.

Preparation Time: 5 minutes
Total Time: 5 minutes
Yield: 1 serving

Ingredients
1 tablespoon peanut butter
1 medium banana, cut into small pieces
2 teaspoon chia seeds
¾ cup almond milk

Method
1.   Combine all ingredients in the tall glass.
2.   Process in the Nutribullet for 10-15 seconds or until smooth and creamy.
3.   Transfer in a serving glass.
4.   Enjoy!

Rehydrating Kombucha Smoothie

This smoothie combines Kombucha, cucumber, lemon and mint. A fresh and delicious blend perfect for those hot summer days. Add a few ice cubes and you've got yourself a drink able to rehydrate you when you most need it.

Preparation Time: 5 minutes
Total Time: 5 minutes
Yield: 1 serving

Ingredients
¾ cup kombucha tea
1 tablespoon lemon juice
1 medium kiwi fruit
1 teaspoon raw sugar
1-2 ice cubes

Method
1.   Combine Kombucha tea, lemon juice, kiwifruit, raw sugar, and ice in the tall glass.
2.   Process in the Nutribullet for 20-30 seconds or until smooth.
3.   Transfer in a serving glass.
4.   Enjoy!

Refreshing Litchi Melon and Coconut Smoothie

Litchi or Lychee is rich in antioxidants and fiber. When combined with coconut water, it yields a light, refreshing and delicious drink, perfect for an energy boost on hot summer days.

Preparation Time: 5 minutes
Total Time: 5 minutes
Yield: 1 serving

Ingredients

5 litchi fruits, peeled and pitted
2/3 cup rock melon, diced
2 tablespoon coconut milk
Coconut water to max line

Method

1.   Combine litchi, rock melon, coconut milk, and coconut water in the tall glass.
2.   Process in the Nutribullet for 20 seconds or until smooth and creamy.
3.   Transfer in a serving glass.
4.   Enjoy!

Kiwi Rock melon and Soy Yogurt Smoothie

Kiwi and melon are not only rich in fiber but they also contain antioxidants that promote wellness.

Preparation Time: 5 minutes
Total Time: 5 minutes
Yield: 1 serving

Ingredients
1 medium kiwifruit, sliced
2/3 cup rock melon, diced
½ cup soy yogurt
Water to max line

Method
1.   Combine kiwifruit, rock melon, soy yogurt, and water in your Nutribullet.
2.   Process for 30 seconds or until smooth and well blended.
3.   Pour in a chilled glass and enjoy.

Raspberry Pear and Almond Smoothie

This smoothie recipe is loaded with antioxidants. A great immune system booster!

Preparation Time: 5 minutes
Total Time: 5 minutes
Yield: 1 serving

Ingredients
½ cup frozen raspberries
1 medium pear, cored and diced
1 tablespoon lemon juice
1 teaspoon stevia
Almond milk to max line

Method
1.   Place raspberries, pear, lemon juice, stevia, and almond milk in a Nutribullet and process for 20-30 seconds or until well blended and smooth.
2.   Pour in a glass of your choice and enjoy.

Radish Beet and Pineapple Blast

The antioxidant content of this beverage is incredibly high and its taste is rather sweet and tangy.

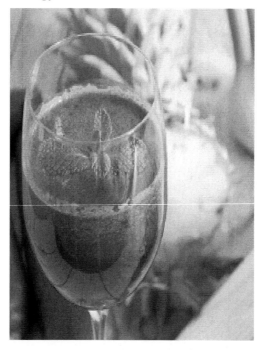

Preparation Time: 5 minutes
Total Time: 5 minutes
Yield: 1 serving

Ingredients

½ medium radish, shredded
½ medium beetroot
¾ cup pineapple, cubed
1 tablespoon lemon juice
Water to max line

Method

1. Combine radish, beetroot, pineapple, lemon juice, and water in your Nutribullet and pulse until well blended and perfectly combined.
2. Pour in your of glass. Garnish with mint or a chunk of pineapple, if desired.
3. Enjoy.

Purple Vegan Smoothie

The name of this smoothie comes from its amazing color, but remembers that when it comes to fruit and veggies, bright colors are the reflection of a high nutritional content. This smoothie is earthy, but delicious and I recommend drinking it without adding any sweeteners because the beet is sweet enough.

Preparation Time: 5 minutes
Total Time: 5 minutes
Yield: 1 serving

Ingredients
1 beetroot, diced
½ cup mixed frozen berries
2 tablespoon rolled oats
1 teaspoon flaxseeds
Almond milk to max line

Method
1.   Place beetroot, mixed berries, oats, flaxseeds, and almond milk in your Nutribullet and pulse until well combined and smooth.
2.   Pour in a glass of your choice. Garnish with berry or mint, if desired.
3.   Enjoy.

Purple Kombucha Smoothie

This smoothie combines the Kombucha with beetroot and wild berries to create a slightly fizzy drink. It is also packed with antioxidants for good health.

Preparation Time: 5 minutes
Total Time: 5 minutes
Yield: 1 serving

Ingredients
1 beetroot, diced
½ cup wild berries
1 tablespoon lemon juice
1 teaspoon maple syrup
Kombucha tea to max line

Method
1.   Combine beetroot, wild berries, lemon juice, maple syrup, and Kombucha tea in your Nutribullet and process for 20-30 seconds until smooth and well blended.
2.   Pour the drink in a chilled glass. Garnish with few berries, and mint.
3.   Enjoy.

Pineapple Spinach and Walnut Smoothie Recipe With Goji Berries

This wonderful green smoothie recipe with pineapple, spinach, walnut, and Goji berries is a nutrient powerhouse. It is loaded with healthy goodness that helps promote optimal health.

Preparation Time: 5 minutes
Total Time: 5 minutes
Yield: 1 serving

Ingredients
1 cup spinach
1 cup pineapple, cut into small cubes
2 tablespoon Goji berries
2 tablespoons walnuts
Water to max line

Method
1.   Place spinach, pineapple, Goji berries, walnuts, and water into the tall glass. Process in the NutriBullet for 10-12 seconds or until combined well.
2.   Pour in a chilled glass. Garnish with a small chunk of pineapple or spinach, if desired.
3.   Serve and enjoy!

Pineapple Kiwi and Parsley Smoothie

This delectable green smoothie recipe made with pineapple, kiwi, parsley, and coconut water is rich in fiber, vitamins and minerals which promote heart and digestive health.

Preparation Time: 5 minutes
Total Time: 5 minutes
Yield: 1 serving

Ingredients

¾ cup pineapple, cubed
1 medium kiwi
1 handful parsley, coarsely chopped
1 teaspoon chia seeds
Coconut water to max line

Method

1.   Combine pineapple, kiwi, parsley, chia seeds, and coconut water in the tall glass. Process in the NutriBullet for 20 seconds or until smooth.
2.   Pour mixture in a serving glass. Garnish with a small chunk of pineapple or parsley sprig, if desired.
3.   Serve and enjoy!

Cardamom Spiced Papaya Soy Smoothie

This mildly spiced smoothie recipe with papaya, soy milk, stevia, and cardamom will surely satisfy your hunger and sweet cravings.

Preparation Time: 5 minutes
Total Time: 5 minutes
Yield: 1 serving

Ingredients

¾ cup papaya, cubed
2/3 cup soy milk
1 teaspoon stevia
¼ teaspoon cardamom, ground
1-2 ice cubes

Method

1.   Place papaya, soy milk, stevia, cardamom, and ice cubes in the tall glass. Process in the NutriBullet for 20-30 seconds or until smooth and creamy.
2.   Transfer mixture in a serving glass. Garnish with diced papaya, if desired.
3.   Serve and enjoy!

Acai Berry Apple and Almond Smoothie Recipe

This healthy smoothie recipe contains a delicious mix of flavors from the Acai berries, apple, almond milk and maple syrup. Acai berries and apples are very rich in fiber, vitamins, minerals and antioxidants that has the ability to fight against free radicals that can cause cell damage and many health risks like cardiovascular disease and cancer.

Preparation Time: 5 minutes
Total Time: 5 minutes
Yield: 1 serving

Ingredients

½ cup Acai Berries
½ medium apples, peeled, cubed
½ cup almond milk
1 teaspoon maple syrup
¼ cup crushed ice

Method

1.   Place Acai berries, apple, almond milk, maple syrup, and ice into the tall glass. Place in the NutriBullet and process for 20 seconds or until blended well.
2.   Pour mixture into a tall glass. Garnish with a few Acai berries, if desired.
3.   Serve immediately to enjoy.

Arugula Strawberry and Soy Smoothie

This is a wonderful green smoothie recipe made with arugula, strawberry, and soy milk. If you want something that will give you a boost this is the right one for you.

Preparation Time: 5 minutes
Total Time: 5 minutes
Yield: 1 serving

Ingredients
1 handful arugula
½ cup frozen strawberries
2/3 cup soy milk, unsweetened
1 teaspoon agave nectar
1-2 ice cubes

Method
1.   Combine arugula, strawberries, soy milk, and agave nectar in the tall glass. Process in the NutriBullet for 20 seconds or until mixture becomes smooth.
2.   Transfer mixture in a serving glass with ice. Garnish with a small strawberry, if desired.
3.   Serve and enjoy!

Acai Berry Banana and Soy Yogurt Smoothie

This awesome smoothie with Acai berries, banana, and soy yogurt will surely energize you as you head out to work or school.

Preparation Time: 5 minutes
Total Time: 5 minutes
Yield: 1 serving

Ingredients
¾ cup acai berries
½ medium banana, peeled, cut into small pieces
½ cup soy yogurt
1 tablespoon wheat germ
Water to max line

Method
1.   Place acai berries, banana, soy yogurt, wheat germ, and water in the tall glass. Puree in the NutriBullet for 20 seconds or until it becomes smooth and creamy.
2.   Pour in a chilled tall glass. Garnish with few acai berries, if desired.
3.   Serve and enjoy!

Acai Berry Banana Strawberry and Soy Smoothie

This is delightful smoothie recipe made with a mix of berries; banana and soy milk is loaded with good for you nutrients to keep you always on the go.

Preparation Time: 5 minutes
Total Time: 5 minutes
Yield: 1 serving

Ingredients

½ cup acai berries

½ cup strawberries, halved

½ frozen medium bananas

½ cup soy milk, plain or vanilla

¼ cup crushed ice

Method

1.   In the tall glass, place the acai berries, strawberries, banana, soy milk, and crushed ice. Process in the NutriBullet for 20 seconds or until smooth.

2.   Pour mixture in a tall glass with ice. Garnish with a few berries or mint sprig, if desired.

3.   Serve and enjoy!

Berry Coconut and Hemp Seed Smoothie

This smoothie is so fragrant and delicious. The berries give it a nice flavor, but let's not forget about its high nutritional content either.

Preparation Time: 5 minutes
Total Time: 5 minutes
Yield: 1 serving

Ingredients

¼ cup raspberries
¼ cup strawberries
2 tablespoons coconut milk
1 teaspoon hemp seeds
½ teaspoon vanilla extract
½ cup coconut water
¼ cup crushed ice

Method

1.   Combine all the ingredients in your Nutribullet and pulse until smooth and creamy.
2.   Pour the smoothie in a glass and garnish with raspberry, if desired.
3.   Enjoy.

Easy Vegan Tropical Smoothie

This healthy smoothie recipe is so delicious and nutritious. It perfect for morning or afternoon snack.

Preparation Time: 5 minutes
Total Time: 5 minutes
Yield: 1 serving

Ingredients

½ medium ripe bananas cut into small
pieces
½ cup pineapple chunks
½ cup mango, cubed
½ cup papaya, cubed
2 tablespoon coconut milk
Coconut water to max line
Ice cubes, to serve

Method

1.   Combine banana, pineapple,
mango, papaya, coconut milk, and coconut
water in your Nutribullet and process for
20 seconds until well blended and
smooth.
2.   Pour in a glass with ice cubes.
3.   Enjoy.

Apple Pumpkin and Coconut Smoothie with Parsley

This rich and nutritious smoothie is a real treat during those cold winter days. Its autumn flavor is comforting and its nutrients will give you an energy boost and also keep you full for a long period of time.

Preparation Time: 5 minutes
Total Time: 5 minutes
Yield: 1 serving

Ingredients

1 medium apple, cored and diced
½ cup pumpkin puree
2 tablespoon pumpkin seeds
¼ teaspoon cinnamon, ground
Coconut water to max line

Method

1.   Combine apple, pumpkin puree, cinnamon, and coconut water in your Nutribullet. Process at least 20 seconds until smooth.
2.   Pour in a serving glass and garnish with parsley.
3.   Enjoy.

Pea Protein Piña Colada Smoothie

A protein-rich smoothie recipe that taste like Piña Colada.

Preparation Time: 5 minutes
Total Time: 5 minutes
Yield: 1 serving

Ingredients
½ cup pineapple chunks
½ medium bananas cut into small pieces
1 scoop pea protein smoothie
¼ cup crushed ice
Coconut water to max line

Method
1.   Place pineapple chunks, banana, pea protein powder, ice and coconut water in a Nutribullet.
2.   Process for 20-30 seconds or until smooth.
3.   Enjoy.

Soy Protein Choco Banana and Chia Smoothie

This protein rich smoothie recipe is made with choco-flavored soy protein powder, banana, and chia seeds. Great smoothie recipe athletes and fitness enthusiasts.

Preparation Time: 5 minutes
Total Time: 5 minutes
Yield: 1 serving

Ingredients

1 medium banana
1 scoop soy protein powder, chocolate flavor
1 teaspoon chia seeds
Water to max line

Method

1.   In the tall glass, place the banana, protein powder, chia seeds, and water. Process in the Nutribullet for 20 seconds or until smooth.
2.   Pour mixture in a serving glass. Garnish with banana slices, if desired.
3.   Enjoy.

Vegan Protein Cherry Orange Smoothie

This a nice twist to your regular protein shakes, it has a perfect blend of flavors and nutrition from the cherries, orange, and vanilla flavored soy protein powder.

Preparation Time: 5 minutes
Total Time: 5 minutes
Yield: 1 serving

Ingredients
8 pieces fresh cherries, pitted
½ medium orange, peeled and cut into segments
1 scoop soy protein powder, vanilla flavor
Water to max line

Method
1.   Combine cherries, orange, soy protein powder, and water in the Nutrilbullet.
2.   Process until smooth. Transfer in a serving glass.
3.   Enjoy.

Almond Papaya and Ginger Vegan Smoothie

If you want a smoothie that will keep your digestive system healthy, this is the one.

Preparation Time: 5 minutes
Total Time: 5 minutes
Yield: 1 serving

Ingredients

¼ cup blanched almonds
¾ cup papaya, diced
2 ice cubes
1 teaspoon fresh ginger, grated
Water to max line

Method

1.   Mix all the ingredients in a Nutribullet and pulse until well blended and smooth.
2.   Pour in a serving glasses and garnish with a small slice of papaya.
3.   Enjoy.

◆

Date Almond and Flaxseed Smoothie

This smoothie has its natural sweetness from the dates. The almonds themselves are rich and healthy, while the dates boost the nutritional content of the smoothie by adding plenty of fiber, vitamins, and minerals.

Preparation Time: 5 minutes
Total Time: 5 minutes
Yield: 1 serving

Ingredients

¼ cup raw almonds, soaked in ½ cup water
½ cup pitted dates
¼ teaspoon vanilla extract
Water to max line

Method

1.   Combine all the ingredients in your Nutribullet and process until smooth and creamy.
2.   Pour the smoothie in a glass of your choice and enjoy.

Spiced Mango Almond Smoothie

This cinnamon-spiced smoothie recipe with mango and almond milk makes a great breakfast or before/after workout snack. Mangoes are an excellent source of vitamin A that fights free radicals in the body.

Preparation Time: 5 minutes
Total Time: 5 minutes
Yield: 1 serving

Ingredients
½ cup mango, diced
2/3 cup almond milk
2 tablespoons wheat germ
¼ teaspoon turmeric, ground

Method
1.   Place mango, almond milk, wheat germ, and cinnamon in the tall glass. Process in the NutriBullet for 20 seconds or until smooth and creamy.
2.   Transfer mixture in a serving glass. Garnish with mango slice, if desired.
3.   Serve and enjoy!

Apple Celery Orange and Chia Smoothie

Both apple and celery are light ingredients but are loaded with antioxidants and have a strong detoxifying effect which promotes optimum health.

Preparation Time: 5 minutes
Total Time: 5 minutes
Yield: 1 serving

Ingredients

1 medium apple, sliced into small pieces
1 celery stalk, sliced into small pieces
½ cup freshly squeezed orange juice
¼ cup crushed ice

Directions

1.   Combine all the ingredients in your Nutribullet and process for 15-20 seconds or until well blended and smooth.
2.   Pour in a glass of your choice and garnish celery.
3.   Enjoy.

Cranberry Lychee Kombucha Smoothie

This is a delightful smoothie recipe that is rich in dietary fiber and many essential nutrients.

Preparation Time: 5 minutes
Total Time: 5 minutes
Yield: 1 serving

Ingredients
½ cup frozen cranberries
3 pcs. Lychee, peeled and pitted
½ cup almond milk
1 teaspoon stevia
Kombucha tea to max line

Method
1. Combine cranberries, lychees, almond milk, stevia, and Kombucha in your Nutribullet and pulse 20 seconds or until smooth and well blended.
2. Pour in a glass and garnish with fresh cranberries.

Minty Apple Pear and Soy Yogurt Smoothie

Apple or pear can be used for this smoothie with the same delicious, comforting result. Add soy yogurt for consistency and some chia seeds for added nutrients and you can say you have a perfect smoothie for breakfast or lunch.

Preparation Time: 5 minutes
Total Time: 5 minutes
Yield: 1 serving

Ingredients

½ medium apple, cored and cut into small pieces
½ medium pear, cored and cut into small pieces
¾ cup soy yogurt
1 mint sprig
Watermax line

Method

1.   Place apple, pear, soy yogurt, mint, and water in your Nutribullet and process until smooth.
2.   Pour in chilled glasses of your choice and garnish with mint, if desired.
3.   Enjoy.

Apple Almond Spinach Smoothie with Pecans

This green smoothie recipe with apple, pecans, almond milk, and spinach is a very nice breakfast or snack item because it can supply your body with the right nutrients it needs to keep you energized and nourished well.

Preparation Time: 5 minutes
Total Time: 5 minutes
Yield: 1 serving

Ingredients
1 medium apple, peeled, cored, and diced
1cup spinach, torn
6 pecan nuts
¾ cup almond milk
Water to max line

Method
1.   Combine apple, spinach, pecans, almond milk, and water in the tall glass. Process in the NutriBullet for 20 seconds or until it becomes smooth.
2.   Pour in a serving glass. Garnish with a small slice of apple, if desired.
3.   Serve and enjoy!

Dragon fruit Mango Rice and Flaxseed Cooler

This smoothie recipe with dragon fruit, mango, rice milk, and flaxseeds is what you should have to start your morning right. It has all the nutrients you need to give you a quick boost of energy.

Preparation Time: 5 minutes
Total Time: 5 minutes
Yield: 1 serving

Ingredients
1 medium dragon fruit, peeled and diced
½ cup ripe mango, diced
2/3 cup rice milk
1 teaspoon flaxseeds
¼ cup crushed ice

Method
1.   Place dragon fruit, mango, rice milk, flaxseeds, and ice in the tall glass. Process in the NutriBullet for 20 seconds or until combined well.
2.   Pour in a serving glass with ice. Garnish with a small slice of dragon fruit or mango, if desired.
3.   Serve and enjoy!

Arugula Banana and Rice Milk Smoothie

This is a wonderful green smoothie recipe made with arugula, banana, and rice milk. If you want something that will give you a boost this is the right one for you.

Preparation Time: 5 minutes
Total Time: 5 minutes
Yield: 1 serving

Ingredients
1 cup arugula
1 medium banana
2/3 cup rice milk, unsweetened
1 teaspoon hemp seeds
½ teaspoon vanilla extract
1-2 ice cubes

Method
1.   Combine arugula, banana, rice milk, hemp seeds, vanilla extract, and ice cubes in the tall glass. Process in the NutriBullet for 20-30 seconds or until mixture becomes smooth.
2.   Transfer mixture in a serving glass with ice. Garnish with a small slice of banana, if desired.
3.   Serve and enjoy!

Honeydew Melon Arugula and Almond Smoothie

This is an awesome green smoothie recipe made with arugula, honeydew melon, and almond milk. Perfect for breakfast or snack on the go.

Preparation Time: 5 minutes
Total Time: 5 minutes
Yield: 1 serving

Ingredients

1 cup honeydew melon, cubed
1 cup arugula
2/3 cup almond milk, unsweetened
1-2 ice cubes

Method

1.   Combine honeydew, arugula, and almond milk in the tall glass. Process in the NutriBullet for 20-30 seconds or until mixture becomes smooth.
2.   Transfer mixture in a serving glass with ice. Garnish with a small slice of melon, if desired.
3.   Serve and enjoy!

Watermelon Lime and Coconut Smoothie

This refreshing smoothie recipe with watermelon, lime, and coconut milk will not only keep you hydrated during summer but nourished as well.

Preparation Time: 5 minutes
Total Time: 5 minutes
Yield: 1 serving

Ingredients
1 cup seedless watermelon, cubed
1 tablespoon lime juice
2 tablespoon coconut milk
1 teaspoon raw sugar
Water to max line

Method
1.   Place watermelon, lime juice, coconut milk, and raw sugar into the tall glass. Process in the NutriBullet for 10-15 seconds or until becomes smooth.
2.   Pour in a chilled serving glass. Garnish with a small chunk of watermelon, if desired.
3.   Serve and enjoy!

Watermelon and Veggie Delight Smoothie Recipe

This delicious low-calorie smoothie recipe with watermelon, lettuce, fennel, lemon juice and honey is a healthy way to satisfy your sweet cravings! Watermelon is 90% water which makes this drink weight-watcher friendly and also it is high in fiber that helps promote healthy digestion. While lettuce, fennel and lemon are detoxifying agents that help remove toxins from the body.

Preparation Time: 5 minutes
Total Time: 5 minutes
Yield: 1 serving

Ingredients

¾ cup watermelon
¼ medium fennel bulb, shredded
2 tablespoon lemon juice
1 teaspoon agave nectar
Water to max line

Method

1.   Place watermelon, fennel bulb, lemon juice, agave nectar, and water into the tall glass. Process in the NutriBullet for 20 seconds or until combined well.
2.   Pour in a chilled glass. Garnish with a slice of watermelon, if desired.
3.   Serve and enjoy!

Pear Banana and Soy Smoothie

This healthy smoothie recipe with pear, banana, lime, and soymilk will provide your body with healthy carbs and antioxidants which promotes healthy body.

Preparation Time: 5 minutes
Total Time: 5 minutes
Yield: 1 serving

Ingredients

1 medium pear, cored and diced
½ medium bananas cut into small pieces
1 tablespoon lime juice
½ cup soy milk
Water to max line

Method

1.   Combine pear, banana, lime juice, soy milk, and water in the tall glass. Process in the NutriBullet for 20 seconds or until smooth.
2.   Pour in a serving glass. Garnish with a slice of lime, if desired.
3.   Serve and enjoy!

Easy Tropical Sunrise Smoothie

This smoothie combines various tropical fruits not only for their amazing taste, but also for their boosted nutritional content. The final drink is highly flavorful and the fragrance of the tropical fruits will flood your senses with deliciousness.

Preparation Time: 5 minutes
Total Time: 5 minutes
Yield: 1 serving

Ingredients

½ cup mango, cubed

½ cup papaya, cubed

½ medium banana, sliced

2 tablespoons coconut milk

Coconut water to max line

Method

1.	Place mango, papaya, banana, coconut milk, and coconut water in your Nutribullet and process until well blended and smooth.

2.	Pour the smoothie in a chilled glass and garnish with a slice of mango or papaya, if desired.

3.	Enjoy.

34383995R00118

Printed in Great Britain
by Amazon